Safe From The Rain

Word Scenery

W. J. Wong

India | USA | UK

Made with ❤ on the BookLeaf Publishing Platform

www.bookleafpub.in

www.bookleafpub.com

Dedication

For the whole world.

Preface

A lot of the time our minds are filled not with long coherent thoughts but flashes of memory, insight, and pain that come and go and come again. Stories, scenes, horror and regret, hope and defiance, feelings, logic, acts of cruelty and mercy. I love writing poetry and short prose because of how it can be used to illustrate how thoughts, quick and vivid, flash one by one through my head in a very different way from other forms of art. I've also always been interested in Greek mythology and mental health, hence "Narcissist" and "the lotus garden." This collection also focuses a little on the experience of women and girls, especially when it comes to interacting with the men in their lives and communities.

Acknowledgements

My mother and father

My ancestors

My mentors

And of course, my darling cats

1. Mommy's Letter, Never Sent

Whatever happened to you, little guy?
How could you be the best thing that ever happened to me
and the worst thing to somebody else?
You have my eyes, but I don't see myself there anymore
My perfect baby boy, six pounds, a little doll
Little guy, so sweet, so shy, so smart and strong
But you're not a child anymore
You'll always be my child
but you are not a child anymore
I think this over and over, trying to make it make sense
Little guy, I wish to God it was me you killed, not her
so that I would not have to see
what kind of person
you've grown up to be

2. Heroes

If he killed you, you'd been a hero
All over the news tomorrow
But since you're a living victim
How could you say that about him?

He's got such a good reputation
Besides those awful allegations
How can we write him away
Just because of what you say?

Why can't we just all get along?
Who can define what's right or wrong?
Let's not pick sides--- but if we do
We like him more than we like you.

3. Pigs

I've really got her
This amazing thing
My daughter, my daughter

My daughter, my daughter
She fell down from heaven
We made her. I caught her.

I thought that I'd got her
She was my baby
So who forgot her?

They got her, they got her
She's crying. She's dying.
My daughter, my daughter

A pig to the slaughter
Just take me, not her
No one would catch her
I've really lost her
My daughter, my daughter

4. A Disturbance

Eavesdropping on the police radios
Calls for *backup.* Domestic disturbance.
Individual well known to authorities.
Barricaded
They need more officers on scene.
Too dangerous, *no chances.*
He will not let them in. Inside,
his wife is dying.
You cannot listen anymore.
Later, you learn
you knew her.

5. Narcissist

The real Narcissus never hurt anyone but himself
and did nothing wrong except to turn down a goddess
who lusted after his beautiful face
He died alone by a reflective forest pool
Spellbound, entrapped, unable to escape
his own captivating expression.
Narcissus, were you tortured as you reached your end?
Did tears fall from your dry eyes
and break up the image of your twin?
Did you come back to sanity for one terrible moment
until the water went still, and you were hypnotized
again?

6. Leap of Faith

Once I made a leap of Faith
With no clue where I'd land
But when I needed to get up
Faith did not lend me a hand

7. Everest

you're at the top
you did the climb

you couldn't stop
the rest? no time

you had to leave
a few behind

can't pause to grieve
one day, they'll find

the sacrificed.
the frozen friends

for now, be proud
you reached the end.

8. One Cold June Evening

A dying garden land
June flowers fade. So cold.
Why is summer icy?
Nothing has gone as planned
Green withers and grows old
Touching a flower, I see
my shaky little hand
is bone now, black with mold
June isn't dead, just me.

9. The Bomb

Like this! All over.
Like that! All done.
Shop closed forever.
I'm gone. You're gone.
Oh well. Boo hoo.
We're done. *Well* done.
I wonder who
Dropped the first one.
Like this, we fry.
Like that, we're cooked.
Oh, how I wish
I hadn't looked.

10. the lotus garden

lotus gardens
trapping our limbs
heavy, heavy heavy
Caramel and honey
our mouths overwhelmed
golden, ripe, seedless
Swollen bellies
pregnant with fruit
eating, eating, eating
our lives fading away
happy but hungry, so hungry
bite by bite
we burned Troy
tricked the Cyclops
escaped Scylla and Charybdis
even outwitted the gods
But the lotus, the lotus
the lotus

11. Her Happiness

My little girl, her happiness
With the little curl on her forehead
It wasn't meant to be like this

When she was born, I thought like this
She'll have the world and more, I said
My little girl, her happiness

I ask myself how could I miss
Her need for more, the text unread?
It wasn't meant to be like this
My little girl's unhappiness

12. Nightly News

Someone attacks me every night
I scream and kick and scratch in terror
Fall out of bed and hit the light
I am the only one who's there

Someone attacks me every night
Hands tight around my throat- no air
I can't see who I have to fight
The lights come on- still no one there

13. Dreaming About the Future

I dreamed the future would be spaceships
Hologram games, lasers, and sleek jumpsuits
Instant communication with live video
Food that appeared with the push of a button
Now that all of these things are true
What I really hope for the future
is a place that will let me and my little one in
Somewhere safe from the rain

14. Elegy for a Friendship

I loved you, my dear, sweet friend, and how
To think when I was so shy and lonely
You were my hero, there to welcome me
To the world of gals and get-togethers
Birthday parties you would throw--surprise!
Messages about men. Well, really, boys.
Your many heartbreaks that I listened to
Males come and go, I thought, but friends don't change
You were much older, I thought you were wise
Surrogate mother, mentor, sister, pal
I guess I felt secure and popular
Grateful for attention or compassion
When did I realize you had turned away?
The popular kids' tables had no room
for me, your friend for almost six whole years
I ask you, is my hair now made of snakes?
Because you turn to stone when I am near
Have you filled your ears with plugs of wax
Lest I say something you don't want to hear?
I mourn the friendship as if it were dead
But I really was dying, and you knew
You knew, you knew, that I was suffering deeply,
Well, I lived anyhow, though our friendship did not
So I learned all that glitters is not gold

and not all friends will survive a true hardship
Are you even relieved that I'm alive?

15. Pop Songs Only Make Things Worse

Can we please get a new word
to replace that one in every song?
The one that is so often heard
that starts off sweet, and ends up wrong
The same word that keeps causing a mess
the same old tragedies retold
The word that he says less and less
as I grow old

16. Buried Treasures

There used to be so many, long ago, or so they say
They were washed away by the ocean or rotted in the
ground,
crumbled, misplaced, stolen for museum displays.

Old ones fade away as they are
stashed, hoarded, renovated, occasionally admired
before being put away again,
out of sight and out of mind.

Real precious things are rare
though expensive ones are everywhere.
Buried away, trashy and cheap,
and when they are found they are special no more.

Relics, masterpieces, historical curiosities, novelties,
antiques
interesting but irrelevant, highly un-modern.
Gold and jewels are nothing compared to
numbers and scores and balances,
Far, far more valuable.

The pirates of the world needn't touch a diamond in their
lives

The beaches are coated in trash.
Loot is buried in white noise and blue screens.
Except …

Sometimes they come back.
Just for a moment,
perhaps for a child, an elder, someone wise and innocent.
The glittering golden statue of Guan Yin raises her hand.
The sun reflects off the white marble and golden top of
the Cairo pyramids.
The Mona Lisa smiles.

17. Hypochondria

Pain deep inside the parts of my body
that doctors are skeptical about
I'm more afraid of nothing being there
than of something being there
I'm afraid of the doctors saying
that I learned everything wrong
And say silly patient, don't you know
Your belly is actually your head!

18. Me Time

I believed in mental health days, so I took one.
Okay, so it turned into a mental health week
And then a mental health month
Then into a mental health year
which turned into a mental health decade.
Eventually, I realized I had to take a mental health life.
So I pack my work laptop and half-done projects
A sandwich for lunch and prescriptions in a suitcase
along with my swimsuit and my passport and sunscreen
Because I anticipate this will be a working holiday

19. Something the Cat Dragged In

"Egad!" they cried out, "What is wrong?
"That's made your face so grim and long?"
"Well," I must ask, "is that a crime?
"My face hurts smiling all the time."
And then they ask me if I'm well.
"No offense, you just look like hell."
"Yes, I am perfectly okay.
"I just don't have makeup today."

20. In the Chair

There was an old woman who lived in a chair.
The staff helped her to walk to stand, to dress, to sit
They helped her to eating and to clean and to go potty
They did this, but they were not her family

The old woman's family was gone.
They helped pay the bills and they helped find the home.
They sent her holiday cards, when they had time.
They did this, but they were not with her when she died.

The old woman was dying in the hospital.
The hospital gave her antibiotics and medicine for her
heart
They sedated her and restrained her and resuscitated her
They did this, but they did not let her die in peace.

The old woman suffered horribly and finally died.
Her soul opened its eyes and looked away from the
scene.
She looked around for the light at the end of the tunnel
and before her stood the angel of death.

The angel held out its hand to the old woman and said
"Let me help you up, grandmother."

The old woman's soul spoke for the first time in many
years.
"My name is Lucy, and I can help myself up, thank you
very much."

And Lucy stood up from the hospital bed
and floated hand in hand with the angel of death into the
hereafter.

21. Cut Me a Break

I'm the judge, the jury, and the executioner.
I'm on trial for my life.
I am the victim, horrifically mistreated.
I am the audience crying out for justice.

I prosecute myself (fantastically).
I defend myself (uninspired, halfhearted).
I testify as an expert witness that I am insane,
dangerous, unstable, degenerate, liable.

I find myself guilty, unanimously,
though I already convicted myself
in the court of public opinion.
I sentence myself to death

I march myself out of the courtroom
Outsides to the gallows I have built
Where I will hang myself.

And at the end of it all,
I drag myself up the stairs.
I put the noose around my neck.

Maybe in the bloodthirsty crowd

there is someone who loves me
crying and begging me to have mercy on myself
If there is, I can't hear them anymore.

But at the very end, I realize
I am the one writing this poem
I get to decide how it ends
So

I write myself a happy ending
The rope snaps, the clouds part
A getaway car appears on the horizon
I pull off my own daring rescue
I give myself my second chance

www.ingramcontent.com/pod-product-compliance
Lightning Source LLC
Chambersburg PA
CBHW070726160726
48003CB00006BA/2399